12
1
2
3
4
5
6
7
8
9
10
11

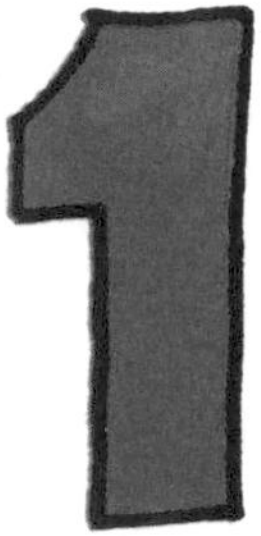
1

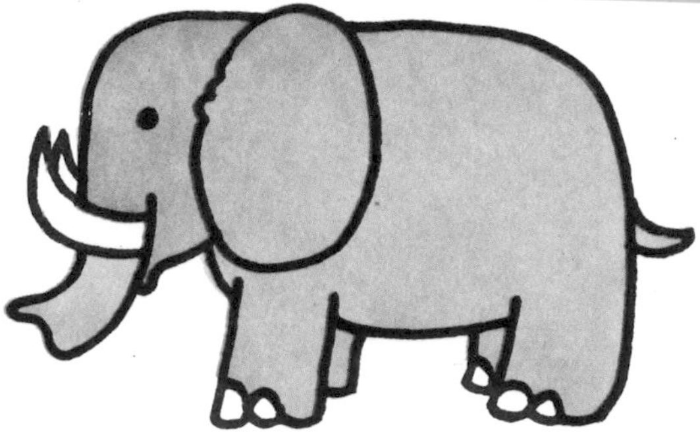

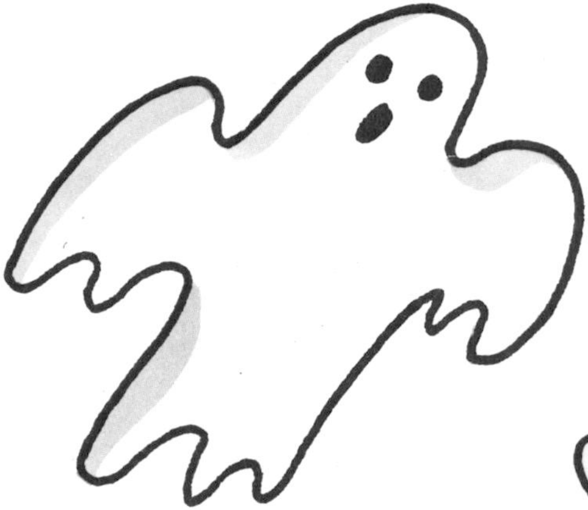

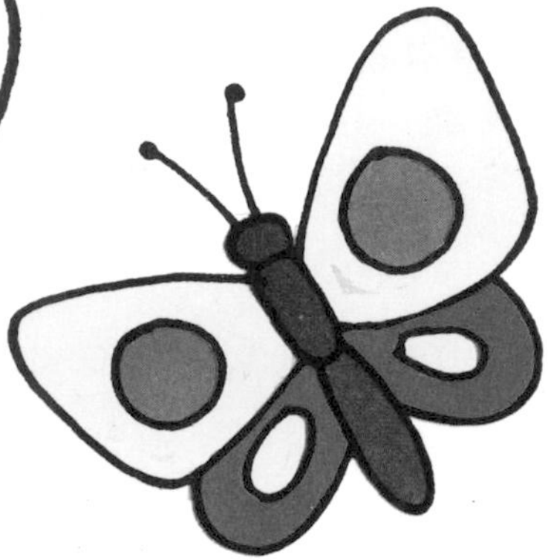

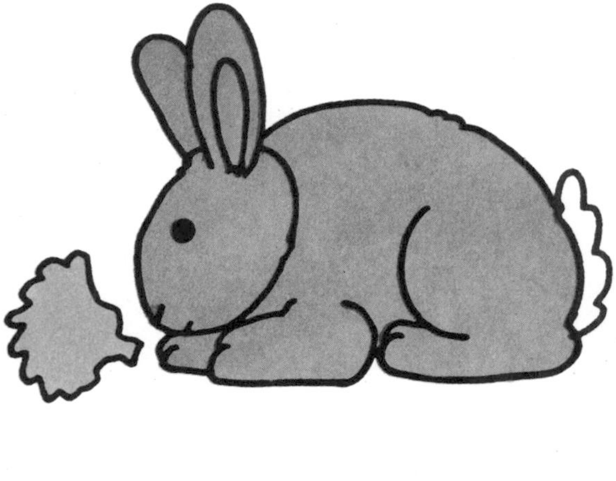

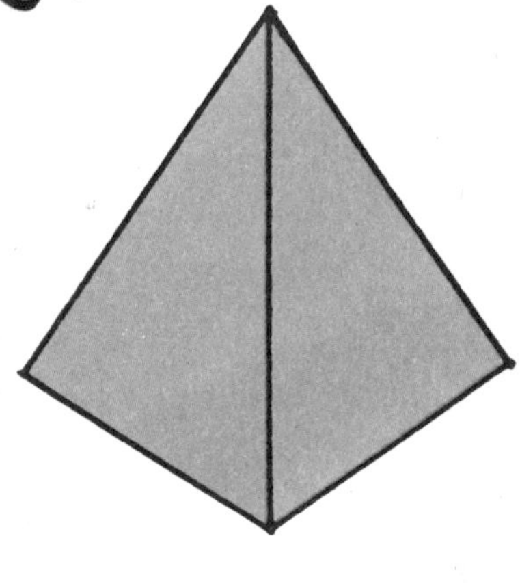

Each book in this series is a thematic collection of words children use, words they see around them, and words for objects with which they are familiar.

Very young children will enjoy talking about the pictures and naming the items. Older children will be able to use the books as reference for their reading and writing, as well as for enjoyment.

Titles in this series

Me and Other People

Everyday Things

At Home

Things That Move

Places to Go

Also available as a Gift Box set

LADYBIRD BOOKS, INC., Lewiston, Maine 04240 U.S.A.
© LADYBIRD BOOKS LTD MCMLXXXVII
Loughborough, Leicestershire, England

Printed in England

everyday things

compiled by LYNNE BRADBURY
illustrated by TERRY BURTON

Ladybird Books

Days of the week

Monday's child is fair of face.

Tuesday's child is full of grace.

Wednesday's child is full of woe.

Thursday's child has far to go.

Friday's child is loving and giving.

Saturday's child works hard for a living.

Sunday

But the child that is born on the Sabbath day, is bonny and blithe and good and gay.

5

Months of the year

January
February
March
April
May
June

July
August
September
October
November
December

Weather

cloud

sun

snow and ice

frost

wind

rain

thunder and lightning

fog

9

Times of day

quarter to seven

dawn

eight o'clock

morning

twelve o'clock

midday

time to get up

time for breakfast

time for lunch

three-thirty

afternoon

five o'clock

evening

quarter past eight

night

time to play

time to watch television

time for bed

Seasons

Spring   warm

Summer   hot

Autumn/Fall   cool

Winter   cold

12

Some places have two seasons.

wet season

dry season

Numbers

1

one elephant

2

two birds

3

three cats

4

four ships

5

five drums

six toadstools

seven apples

eight flowers

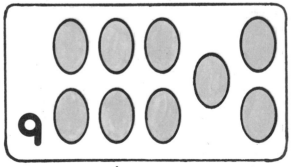

nine eggs

ten bottles

15

Shapes and colors

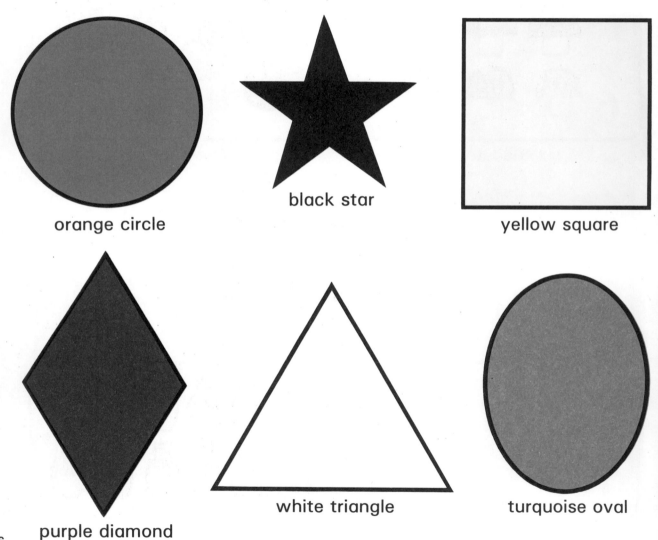

orange circle

black star

yellow square

purple diamond

white triangle

turquoise oval

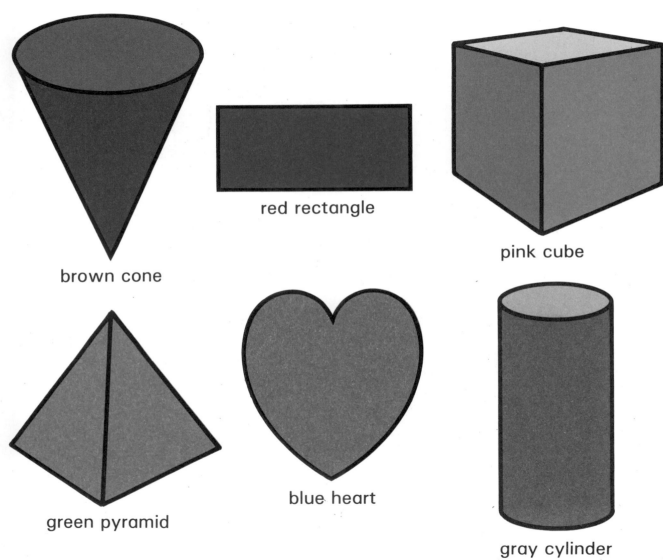

brown cone

red rectangle

pink cube

green pyramid

blue heart

gray cylinder

17

Pets

rabbit

turtle

guinea pig

kitten

cat

fish

mouse

puppy

dog

parakeet

pony

hamster

Birds

duck

duckling

swan

cygnet

hen

chick

rooster

turkey

blackbird

crow

swallow

robin

thrush

pigeon

flamingo

eagle

owl

21

Small creatures

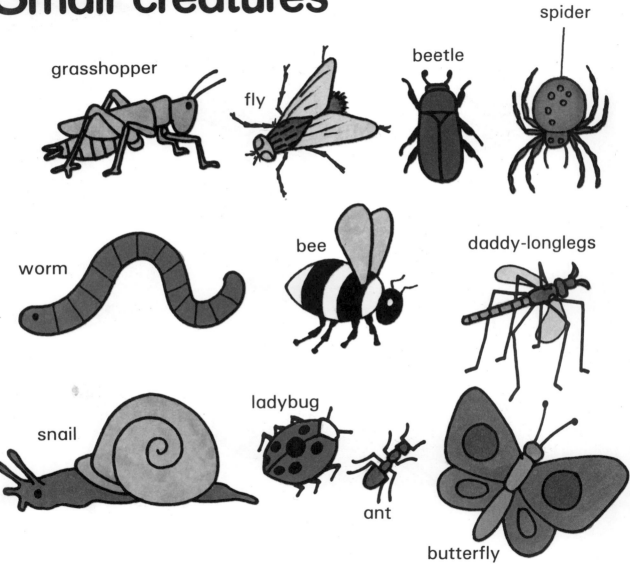

grasshopper

fly

beetle

spider

worm

bee

daddy-longlegs

snail

ladybug

ant

butterfly

Flowers

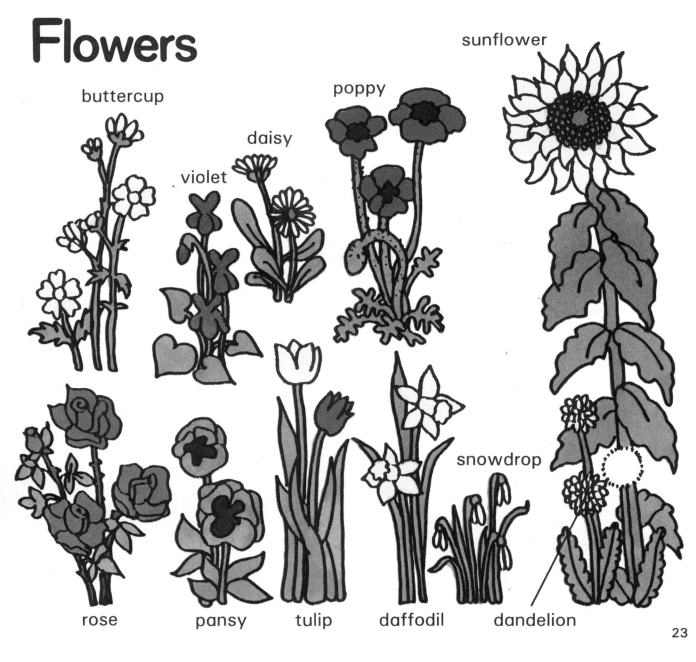

buttercup

poppy

sunflower

daisy

violet

snowdrop

rose

pansy

tulip

daffodil

dandelion

23

Musical instruments

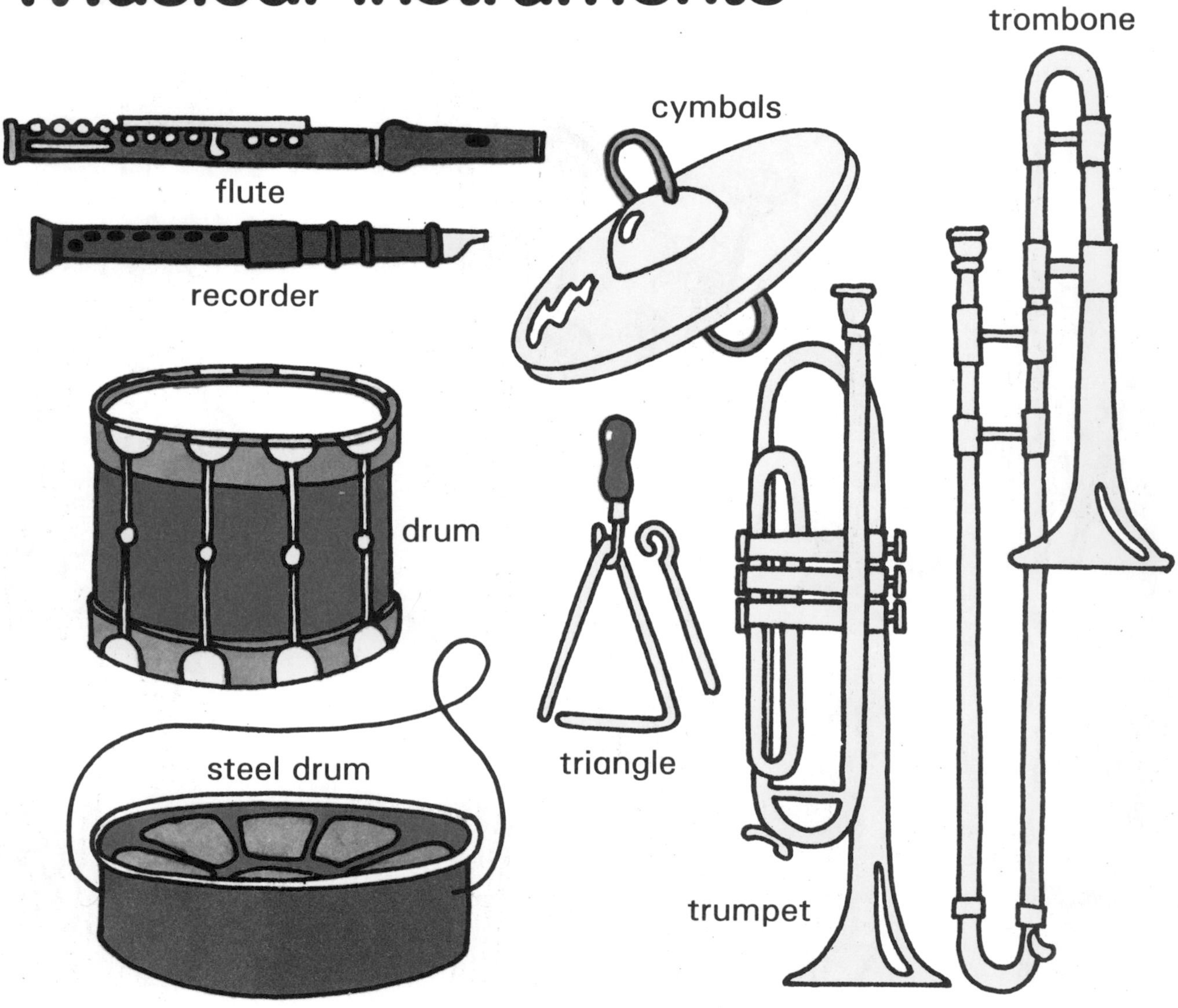
flute
recorder
cymbals
trombone
drum
triangle
steel drum
trumpet

violin

tambourine

cello

guitar

banjo

piano

Story words

ghost

castle

dragon

prince

princess

witch

wand

fairy

giant

wizard

broomstick

spell

dwarf

cauldron

27

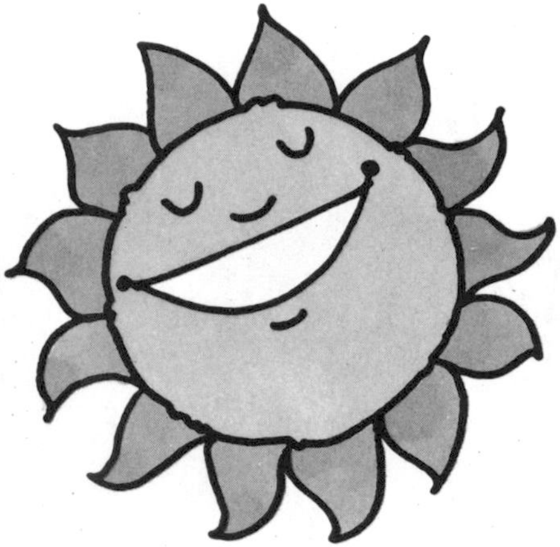

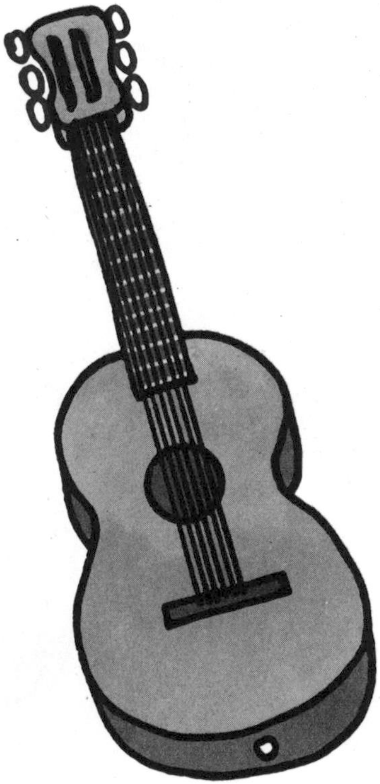

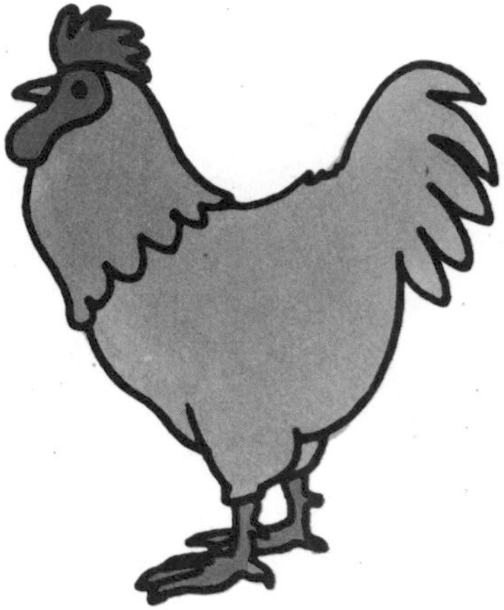

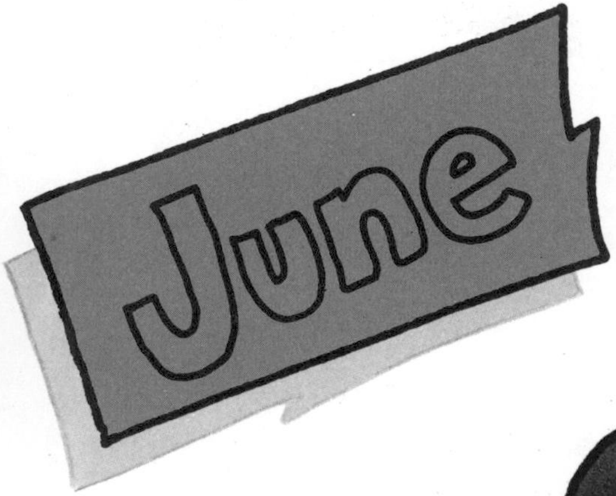
June

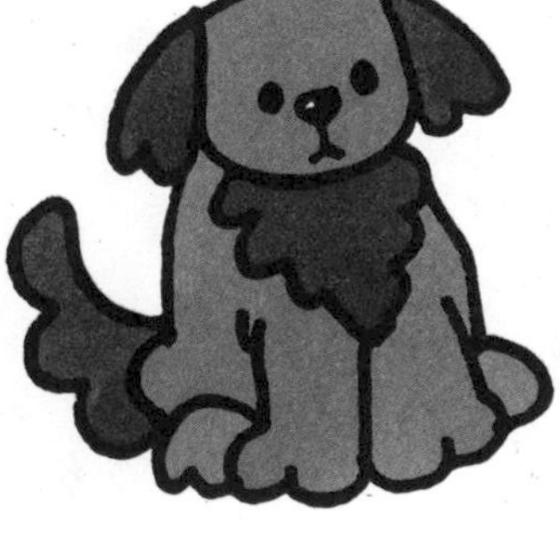

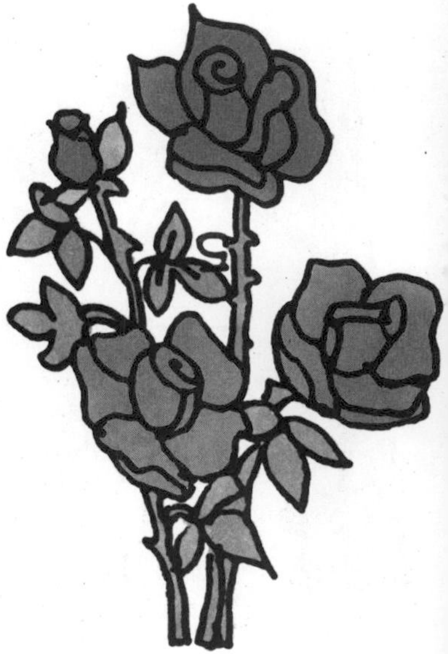